Forced Marriage

Forced Marriage

A Study on British Bangladeshi Community

Abu Sadik Maruf

authorHOUSE®

AuthorHouse™
1663 Liberty Drive
Bloomington, IN 47403
www.authorhouse.com
Phone: 1-800-839-8640

Published by AuthorHouse   04/17/2012

ISBN: 978-1-4678-8925-4 (sc)
ISBN: 978-1-4678-8926-1 (e)

To
The Victims of Forced Marriage

Contents

Preface

Forced marriage is of current national and international importance as a social problem. It is a marriage without 'free and voluntary consent' of one or both of the intending spouses. The pressure put on people to marry against their will can be physical and emotional. I have seen how people regardless of age and gender are forced into marriage in the name of family honour, tradition and religion. The placement during my first degree in Social Work introduced me with different types of violence against women and children including forced marriage. Later, I have attended postgraduate courses that strongly discuss the impact of ethnic, religious and cultural factors on women. Throughout my University life, there were presentations, seminars and discussions also on the role of social work in minimising social problems including domestic violence and other gender based issues. I, therefore, as a learner in the field of social work, thought that it would be interesting and useful to study this issue of forced marriage.

This book is based on a qualitative empirical research—*An Evaluation of Existing Social Work Services on Forced Marriage: a Study on British Bangladeshi Community* that was undertaken in 2010 and was submitted in 2011 to the University of East London in partial fulfilment of the requirements for the award of MA in International Social Work and Community Development. However, the respondents of the research have appreciated by saying that the study itself is a wonderful way to engage and educate people about forced marriage. They also strongly suggested to publish it as it could be an important piece of information to the victims and potential victims of forced marriage. This is the main motivation of the publication. Besides, the front-line practitioners and support workers dealing with violence against women including forced marriage may also find it useful. Academics and students in Social Sciences may gain more knowledge about the concept and find the limitations or gaps that will lead to further studies on the subject. Above all, people from concerned communities may become more active to abolish this bad custom.

Thanks to **Karen Adshead**, my supervisor at the University, who helped with her experience to conduct the study. I am indebted to **all the interviewees** for their insights and views, and for giving their valuable time for the research project. Without their participation and involvement the project could not have been completed. I am very grateful to the **survivors** who have reminded dreadful past for the benefit of my study. I would like to extend my thanks to **all relevant organisations** for patiently responding to all my questions and queries. My special thanks to the government's **Forced Marriage Unit** for their support during the study.

Finally, I like to express my warm love and thanks to all of them who contributed during the study and later in publication. All responsibilities for errors and omissions lie with me as the author of this book.

List of Abbreviations

BAME—Black Asian and Minority Ethnic
BHC—British High Commission
CLU—Community Liaison Unit
CP—Child Protection
DLR—Discretionary Leave to Remain
DV—Domestic Violence
ELR—Exceptional Leave to Remain
FCO—Foreign and Commonwealth Office
FM—Forced Marriage
FMPO—Forced Marriage Protection Order
FMU—Forced Marriage Unit
IDVA—Independent Domestic Violence Adviser
ILE—Indefinite Leave to Enter
ILR—Indefinite Leave to Remain
LGBT—Lesbian Gay Bisexual and Trans-gendered
NGO—Non-governmental Organisation
NRPF—No Recourse to Public Funds
PBUH—Peace Be Upon Him
SPSS—Statistical Package for the Social Sciences

List of Tables

Abstract

This book mainly is the report of a qualitative empirical study on forced marriage in the UK. To know the nature and types of existing social work services and to evaluate the success and limitations of those, the research was conducted on the British Bangladeshi community. First of all, it focused on the circumstances of forced marriage to investigate the cultural issues relating to forced marriage and finds out the major causes. Then it examined the available services for the victims and survivors of forced marriage and preventive activities initiated by the relevant organisations. Finally, an evaluation attempted to understand the success and limitations of existing services answered the research question. The study used interviews and survey as methods of data collection under largely a qualitative approach with a small statistical analysis. As the issue of forced marriage is multidimensional, a number of perspectives accommodating gender, ethnicity, social class and religion were undertaken as a theoretical framework for the analysis and discussion of the findings.

The study clearly defined forced marriage as 'marriage without free and full consent' and differentiated it from arranged marriage. Interestingly, all arranged marriages are not forced marriages but all forced marriages are arranged. Stronger relation build up within kinship ties and preventing relationships outside the ethnic, cultural, and religious groups are some of the main reasons behind forced marriage. Homophobia, controlling unwanted behaviour and sexuality are emerging as other major causes of forced marriage. As majority people are Muslim in this community, Muslim identity also becoming more significant than ethnic identity. However, the study revealed that one fifth of total victims is from

British Bangladeshi community and most of them are 18-22 years old female. Despite the excellent work of the Forced Marriage Unit and others, support services are still not effective enough to abolish the practice. Participants in this study, strongly favoured responses should include better support services for victims, community education and awareness. It is also important to ensure adequate strategic planning at local level and training for front-line practitioners. The key to this problem lies within the communities themselves and therefore, the government must be guided by these communities. It provides the national context of forced marriage and a set of recommendations to minimise limitations and maximise the support to the victims.

Chapter 1

Introduction

1.1 Background

Forced marriage is recognised as a form of violence against women and children that suffers men also. It is a serious abuse of human rights. Studies showed that victims can be as young as 9 years old to older as 35 and over. Even in the UK, hundreds of people, particularly girls and young women are forced into marriage each year.

> *"The Forced Marriage Unit dealt with over 1600 reports*
> *of possible forced marriage in 2009,*
> *375 of which became cases."*
> —Ministry of Justice, 2010: 6

It is found that some victims are taken overseas to marry while others may be married in the UK. There has been much focus on Pakistani, Bangladeshi and Indian communities with regard to forced marriage, and therefore a wider recognition of the issue. It is important to recognise, however, that a wide range of other minority ethnic, religious as well as majority communities are also involved, including African, Middle Eastern, Latin American. Also to a lesser extent forced marriage is visible in Eastern Europeans, Albanian, Chinese, Jewish, and some Christian groups, including Mormon, Jehovah's Witness and Greek Orthodox (Chantler, Gangoli & Hester, 2009).

However, the study focused on the available social work services for the victims and survivors of forced marriage. To evaluate the effectiveness of existing services the research was conducted on British Bangladeshi community.

1.2 Interest and Motivation behind the Research

The author was studying his MA in International Social Work and Community Development that is designed to analyse social work and community development practice and policy throughout the world. It helps the social workers to know about the various social problems and their relation to particular cultures along with national and international policies. While studying, the researcher attended courses that strongly discuss the impact of ethnic, religious and cultural factors on women. There were some presentations also on gender based issues including the author's two: 'Social Work in Minimising Violence against Women in Bangladesh' and 'Cultural Barriers to Gender Equality in Bangladesh'. All of these presentations and discussions encouraged him to study such an issue of forced marriage.

In addition, as an insider, he experienced that because of the appeal to traditional values, attempts to forced marriage often receive support from a wider circle of relatives, friends and acquaintances within the community. While living in Bangladesh, he found most of the British Bangladeshis go there for holiday with their children and some of them arrange marriages without children's consent.

So his observation and experience suggested him that the issue of forced marriage should be studied from different angles.

1.3 Research Question and Hypothesis

The purpose of the study was to know the nature and types of existing social work services and their effectiveness to minimise forced marriage through British Bangladeshi community.

1.4 Aims and Objectives

Following were the aims and objectives of the research conducted on forced marriage.

1. To understand the circumstances of forced marriage through British Bangladeshi community;
   i) to investigate the cultural issues relating to forced marriage,
   ii) to find out the causes behind forced marriage.
2. To know the existing social work services available for the victims of forced marriage;
   i) to find out the available services for the victims and survivors of forced marriage,
   ii) to find out the preventive activities to protect the potential victims of forced marriage.
3. To evaluate the available social work services;
   i) to identify the success and limitations of existing social work services,
   ii) to get some recommendations from the service providers and beneficiaries.

1.5 Rationale for the Research Approach and Methods Chosen

Here, rationale is the logical basis of the research approach and the methods chosen for the study. Consistency was important as this study will be evaluated by others. Therefore, research methods and analysis should be consistent with the analytical approach, guidelines and criteria for data analysis.

The study was being conducted to illuminate the complex and multidimensional nature and causes of forced marriage and to illustrate the success and limitations of social work practice. Because of limited time and resources, the project could only deal with the one community. British Bangladeshi community was chosen to study the circumstances of forced marriage assuming that this community would be able to represent the picture of the whole. Furthermore, as an insider the researcher thought it would be easy to access and constructive data could be collected. After identifying and articulating the research question it guided to follow the chosen methods to collect necessary data. The main interest of the study was in the statements of particular groups of people including their personal views, perceptions and experiences on forced marriage. It was thought that related organisations also could help a lot to find the data that would answer the research question.

However, some significant studies in this area were considered before choosing the research methods under a particular research approach. All of those studies have used such types of methods so were chosen for this study and was expected to produce an important piece of research. Previous studies focused broadly on the concept of forced marriage among various communities and tried to find solution. This research mainly focused on a particular community to know the circumstances of forced marriage in general and then evaluated the existing services.

Chapter 2

Literature Review

2.1 Context

Forced marriage is a social problem. It is a marriage that conducted without the full and free consent of either people or any one of them. Before defining forced marriage need to talk about marriage in general. Marriage is an interpersonal relationship with governmental, social or religious recognition. Merriam-Webster dictionary defines marriage as the following—

"*(1)*: the state of being united to a person of the opposite sex as husband or wife in a consensual and contractual relationship recognised by law, *(2)*: the state of being united to a person of the same sex in a relationship like that of a traditional marriage <same-sex *marriage>*" (Sources:http://mw1.m-w.com/dictionary/marriage).

The first one is accepted all over the world where the second one is accepted only in some parts of the world. However, a general definition of marriage is: a social contract between two individuals that unites their lives legally, economically and emotionally. People marry for many reasons, including one or more of the following: legal, social, emotional, economical, spiritual, and religious. These might include family obligations, the legal establishment of a nuclear family unit, legal protection of children, public declaration of commitment, to obtain citizenship etc. Whatever the reason is people should enter into marriage voluntarily as it is known from the definition that in marriage people share their life together with mutual care and respect.

But in forced marriage, one or both of the people involved are forced into a marriage against their will and without their permission. In forced marriage, at least one party does not consent to the marriage and some elements of duress are involved. The pressure put on people to marry against their will can be physical or emotional. The definition of forced marriage agreed by the Home Office Working Group on Forced Marriage declared forced marriage as "a marriage conducted without the valid consent of both parties, where duress is a factor" (Forced Marriage Unit, 2000: 10). A marriage must be entered into with the full and free consent of both people. The two people involved should feel that they have a choice. If this term is analysed under the concept of Human Rights it finds the same statement as above—"Marriage shall be entered into only with the free and full consent of the intending spouses" {Universal Declaration of Human Rights, Article 16(2)}. Forced marriage is an attack on a person's human rights that promotes unhappiness, depression, fear, self harm and in some cases suicide.

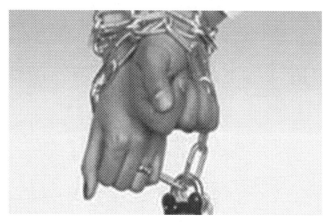

Figure-1: Forced Marriage[1]

However, some people mix up the concept of forced marriage with those known as arranged marriage. But an arranged marriage is not the same as a forced marriage. Now it's relevant to have a look on that. In an arranged or assisted marriage, the families take a role in choosing and introducing the marriage partners (FMU, 2000). In an arranged marriage, families choose the marriage partners on the basis of their own socio-economic status but it depends on the bride and bridegroom whether to marry or not. So there is a right of choice. In traditional arranged marriage, parents arrange for a spouse. If their children do not agree, the parents usually respect their children's wishes and look for another partner. In this type of situation, an all-out attempt to convince their children about the value of the arrangement used to make by the parents without force. In modern age, parents may still engage in some persuasion tactics, but their children's happiness is their priority, so there is a lot of emphasis on the children's feelings, beliefs and convictions and their choices. But still there can be a 'slippage' or blurring between arranged and forced marriage, as some people pointed out: 'parents will arrange the marriage and if children reject the person they will force them to marry the person'. So not only consent is essential to all marriages but also there should not be any sort of pressure.

In 1999, Mike O'Brien, the Minister for Community Relations, set up a working group (chaired jointly by Lord Ahmed of Rotherham and Baroness Uddin of Bethnal Green) to investigate the extent of forced marriage in England and Wales and present proposals for tackling it effectively. Its report, *A Choice by Right* (2000), clarified the key issues regarding forced marriage. After a decade, it is now possible to conclude that it succeeded in establishing a broad consensus on forced marriage within Britain. Following the publication of the report, the Foreign and Commonwealth Office (FCO) established a Community Liaison Unit (CLU) to take forward the working group's recommendations. The CLU was absorbed into a joint FCO-Home Office Forced Marriage Unit (FMU) in 2005 (Khanum, 2008). Later, the Liberal Democrat peer, Lord Lester, sought to extend the range of protection available by introducing the Forced Marriage (Civil Protection) Bill as a Private Member's Bill in November 2006. Then the bill was supported by the government and has now been passed as the Forced Marriage (Civil Protection) Act 2007. The aim of the Act is to provide protection to those at risk of forced marriage and to provide recourse for those who have already been forced into marriage. The Act also sends out a strong signal that forced marriage is unacceptable and will not be tolerated.

FMU deals with 250-300 cases per year (Khanum, 2008). These are the number of most difficult cases. Many more, perhaps thousands of them, are not reported. Historically, forced marriage was common among all communities. Over the course of the twentieth century, the use of force in marriage has become less common within the white British community as a result of changes in relationships between parents and children, and between men and women. In the UK, forced marriage has a deep involvement with some cultures, specifically South Asian and Muslim communities (Oprea, 2005). A record showed that 65% of the cases handled by the FMU are from families of Pakistani origin, **25% of Bangladeshi origin** and the remaining 15% of other origins (Khanum, 2008). Nevertheless, forced marriage is not simply an Asian issue, but has to be tackled within the wider context of evolving relationships between men and women, and between parents and children, across all communities, to build a 'culture of common human rights'.

It has also been suggested that forced marriage is a product of immigration rather than a 'tradition' exported from the country of origin (Phillips & Dustin, 2004:543). It is true that South Asian communities are the largest ethnic minorities in the UK. Among them Bangladeshis are its youngest and fastest-growing community. According to the experimental statistics 2007 (on the basis of National census 2001) 353,900[2] Bangladeshis living in England. Current estimates suggest that there are about 500,000[3] Bangladeshis residing in the UK. Bengalis had been present in Britain as early as the 19th century. The records of first arrivals from the region what is known today as Bangladesh (was British India), were Sylheti cooks in London during 1873, part of the East India Company, who arrived to the UK as lascars in ships to work in restaurants.[4]

Author Caroline Adams records that in 1925 a lost Bengali man was searching for other Bengali settlers in London. These first few arrivals started the process of 'chain migration' mainly from one region of Bangladesh—Sylhet, which led to substantial numbers of people migrating from rural areas of the region, creating links between relatives in Britain and the region (Thapan, 2005). On the other hand, the rates of marriage among Bangladeshis are comparatively higher than some other ethnic minorities in the UK. The governing principle of marital choice for this community is the selection of a partner from a similar social background from the same region. It has also a strong relation with class, religion, age and education.

Katy Gardner, in *Global Migrants: Local Lives* which is an ethnographic study of Talukpur (a Sylheti village community) notes that kinship is "one of the principal factors of social, political and economic organisation in Talukpur as elsewhere in rural Bangladesh" (1995:28-29). The implication of her data for migration to Britain is that marriage is a link between British migrants and a wider network of families across Sylhet.

Marriage is popular amongst Bangladeshis along with some other South Asian communities and religion is an important factor for the high rates of marriage. Marriages are primarily endogamous and are used to reinforce kinship, networks and group boundaries. It is used as an important tool in maintaining the cultural distinctiveness of the group and is very closely related to issues of identity and belonging. Marriage is conducted between sub-groups within these community categories and is associated with social divisions based on family (*Ghusti*), kinship ties (*Khandhan*), caste or caste-like groups (*zat*) and clan (*Bongsho*). Caste hierarchy and status competition between families are important factors in understanding families' motivation for marriage. Women's behaviour, dowries and marriage agreements are all linked to notions of family honour.

On the other hand, when it's about South Asian community, religion of Islam comes as an important factor. Almost all the studies on forced marriage found that it is being practised in Muslim communities largely than others. Although Islam prohibited force into marriage, misinterpretation of Islam along with religious and cultural tradition of particular communities made it quite common in Muslim communities. If someone studies the Islam s/he will find how the base of Islam—Qur'an and Hadith condemn forced marriage. Some people even often raise the question about the rights of women in Islam and it is also true that record of FMU shows around 85% of victims in forced marriage are women (Khanum, 2008). So it is better to consider this issue from women's perspective to see how Islam gives priorities to women in marriage and discourage forced marriage in general.

First of all, need to know how marriage is defined in Qur'an (the noble book for Muslims). Marriage is a sacred bond between a couple, which makes each other permissible for them to enjoy and live happily. Allah (the God for Muslims) has described this eternal and natural relationship between couple, which is filled with security, love, understanding and compassion:

> *"And among His signs is this that He created for you mates from among yourselves, that you may dwell in tranquility with them, and He has put love and mercy between your hearts: Verily in that are signs for those who reflect."*
> —Qur'an, 30:21

The Qur'an also reminds Muslims that a husband and a wife are garments of each other, protecting and complementing each other: ". . . They are a garment for you and you are a garment for them . . ." (Qur'an, 2:187). Arranged marriages are allowed and promoted in Islam as long as they are accepted by both of the partners. One of the conditions for the 'Nikah' (marriage) to be valid is both the man and woman are asked independently of each other as to whether they agree with the marriage or not. If either of them says 'no' then the 'Nikah' cannot continue. Muhammad (PBUH), the last messenger of Allah (God), gave the strictest orders with relation to the rights of others. He said—

> *"Truly Allah has totally forbidden disobedience (and the subsequent hurt) to mothers, burying alive daughters, with-holding the rights of others, and demanding that which is not your right."*
> —Hadith Muslim 4257; recorded by Mughirah B. Shuba

The parents have a responsibility to ensure that both couples are compatible and do not arrange a marriage merely for their own social or personal reasons and they should not blame there children to obey them in such cases. Abu Hurayrah reported Allah's last messenger (PBUH) as having said:

> *"A woman without a husband (or divorced or a widow)*
> *must not be married until she is consulted, and a virgin*
> *must not be married until her permission is sought."*
> —Kitab Al-Nikah, book 008, number 3303

This line indicates that Islam gives full right to women to accept or reject a marriage proposal regardless of her marital status e.g., whether she is a virgin, divorced or widow. Again, narrated Abdullah ibn Umar: "The Prophet (PBUH) said: Consult women about (the marriage of) their daughters" (Kitab Al-Nikah, book 11, number 2090). Islam tells people to consult with mothers so that they can understand and talk to their daughters friendly. Finally, it is found that forced marriages are completely contradictory to the message of Islam. The verses of the Qur'an, the highest Islamic textual authority, say that marriage is solely based on mutual consent of a man and a woman, which makes forced marriages absolutely unacceptable and non-Islamic:

> *"O ye who believe! Ye are forbidden to inherit women*
> *against their will. Nor should you treat them with*
> *harshness, that ye may take away part of the dower you*
> *have given them,—except where they have been guilty*
> *of open lewdness; on the contrary live with them on a*
> *footing of kindness and equity. If ye take a dislike to*
> *them it may be that ye dislike a thing, and Allah brings*
> *about through it a great deal of good."*
> —Qur'an, 4:19

2.2 Key Studies and their Methodologies

Some analytical research reports were the key studies for this research on forced marriage. 'Forced Marriage in the UK: Religious, Cultural, Economic or State Violence?' is a research paper by Chantler, Gangoli and Hester published in 2009. This paper discusses some key issues namely human rights, issues of culture and gender and UK immigration policy in relation to forced marriage. The study used a qualitative approach employing a variety of methods such as different types of interviews, survey, focus group discussions.

There is another significant paper on forced marriage, 'Forced Marriage: Prevalence and Service Response' by Kazimirski, Keogh, Kumari, Smith, Gowland and Purdon with Khanum published in 2009. It aimed to inform policy across government and to feed into new guidelines supporting statutory responsibility for forced marriage. Their methodology had four components: literature review, mapping study, quantitative data sourcing and analysis exercise and a qualitative case study element. The study explores that whilst FM is not exclusively an issue for Asian communities, 97% of those seeking help or advices relating to FM from local organisations were identified as Asian (Kazimirski et al., 2009). In their findings, forced marriage training appears to be core or mandatory for any group of professionals.

'Forced Marriage, Family Cohesion and Community Engagement: National Learning through a Case Study of Luton' is outcome of one of three national pilots funded by the Home Office. The report by Dr Nazia Khanum OBE, published in 2008, highlights the important role played by local community support groups. This was a qualitative study, using Luton as a case study to investigate the key issues relating to forced marriage and so called 'honour'-based violence. It was based on the following methodology: Literature review and collection of information on population, interviewing, group discussions and case studies.

'Community Perceptions of Forced Marriage' studied by Samad and Eade is an analytical report for the Community Liaison Unit (CLU) published in 2002. This report provides the context, explores the problems and the perceptions of forced marriages in the Pakistani and Bangladeshi communities. Evidence was collected from a variety of sources. Statistical data was collated from various population surveys, both national and local; to establish the key demographic changes affecting both communities during the last twenty years. But primary data was collected by one to one interviews with gatekeepers and focus group discussions.

2.3 Theoretical Framework for the Discussion

A theoretical framework is a collection of interrelated concepts. It is like a theory but not necessarily so well worked-out. It guides the research, determining what things the researcher will measure, and what statistical relationships she or he will look for. Problems cannot be articulated except within a conceptual system. No inquirer can investigate a problem from all perspectives simultaneously, and that is why a theoretical framework is necessary. It establishes a vantage point, a perspective, a set of lenses through which the researcher views the problem. However, the issue of forced marriage can be approached from a number of theoretical perspectives. Different analytical approaches produce results that emphasise a particular aspect of the issue. The concern here is that the issue of forced marriage is multidimensional so the author had to engage with a number of perspectives.

The perspective of 'gender' is central to the issue of forced marriage, in particular with women. Ethnic boundaries are often dependent on gender attributes organised around sexuality, marriage and the family. The gender approach sees forced marriages as symptomatic of wider issues associated with domestic violence. It is inextricably associated with control of women, especially their sexuality. Feminists believe that women are oppressed simply due to their sex based on the dominant ideology of patriarchy. Lack of - education, empowerment and consciousness about their human rights to justice, equality and freedom in women - made them more vulnerable to come across any sort of domestic violence including forced marriage. But it is also true that forced marriages are not only about women—they also affect men and gender variations need to be accommodated.

Secondly, an 'ethnic' perspective would locate the phenomenon within the wider context of arranged marriage, especially endogamous marriage. Forced marriage could, therefore, be seen as an extreme extension of endogamy practices and not the result of arranged marriage. Forced marriage could be a cultural distinctiveness of the group and is very closely related to issues of identity and belonging. Particular cultural practices could affect this issue largely. At the same time, immigration can be considered here. Because forced marriage could work as a link between British migrants and a wider network between their ethnic groups living back home.

Third perspective examines the issue in terms of 'social class'. Here need to be aware that the relationship between social class and ethnicity is problematic and that multiple factors need to be built into the concept of social class (Smith et al., 2000). If forced marriage is located within the category of domestic violence than evidence shows that domestic violence takes place across class lines. Caste hierarchy and status competition between families on the basis of social class are important factors in understanding families' motivation for such marriages. Cultural tradition can affect this issue also.

Finally, as religion is one of the most powerful and influential forces in human society, a perspective to understand the issues regarding forced marriage through examining religion and its influence would be beneficial. Religion has shaped people's relationship and behaviour influencing family, community, economic and political life. In this study, it would be the religion of Islam as the focused community and problem closely related with Muslim communities.

This theoretical framework was undertaken as a conceptual map to the investigation.

---

[1] **The picture is collected from the official website of Foreign and Commonwealth Office and can be found on** http://www.fco.gov.uk/en/travel-and-living-abroad/when-things-go-wrong/forced-marriage/

[2] **This statistics is taken from the official website of 'Office for National Statistics'**—http://www.neighbourhood.statistics.gov.uk

[3] **This statistics is based on survey of a Bengali TV channel called 'Channel S' and can be found on their website**—http://www.chsuk.tv

[4] **This information is taken from an online article "Bengali-speaking community in the port of London" available on PortCities UK**—http://www.portcities.org.uk

Chapter 3

Methodology

3.1 Research Approach

The nature of forced marriage indicates that individuals experiencing such marriages are a 'hard to reach' group. This makes it extremely difficult to develop accurate measures of the service responses of forced marriage or to obtain reliable quantitative information. It was decided, therefore, that the study should use largely a qualitative approach along with a small quantitative paradigm employing a variety of methods that would enable exploration of the research question. It was believed that this approach could generate rich data on issues related to forced marriage, and also could examine the research question from different angles. The qualitative approach tends to focus on exploring, in as much detail as possible, smaller numbers of instances which are seen as being interesting and aims to achieve 'depth' rather than 'breadth'.

3.2 Sampling

Sampling is the probabilistic, systematic and judgemental selection of a sub-element from a larger population, with the aim of approximating a representative picture of the whole. It is the practice of choosing a subset of population elements to study instead of the entire population.

The following two non-probability samplings were used in this research:

3.2.1 Purposive sampling—purposive sampling is done when the sample is selected by keeping a certain purpose in mind and researcher tries to include certain individuals or organisations into the study. In this research, purposive sampling were chosen because of i) the sample was an accurate or near to accurate representation of the population, ii) the results were expected to be more accurate, iii) it was less time consuming, iv) it was less expensive, v) lack of personnel, vi) better understanding of language and expressions, vii) thought that worthy data can be collected from this place. For survey, required numbers of organisations were selected purposively from the list of organisations identified through desk research. Again, in familiarisation and stakeholders interviews, people from different social and professional backgrounds were selected purposively. The characteristics of individuals were used as the basis of selection, and therefore chosen to reflect the diversity and breadth of the sample population.

3.2.2 Snowball sampling—Snowball sampling is something as building up a sample through informants. Snowballing, where respondents tell the researcher about others they know with the same or specified characteristics is a method also used in qualitative research. In this research, survivors were identified through snowball sampling. It was useful because researcher was trying to reach populations that were inaccessible or hard to find.

3.3 Sources of Information

3.3.1 Primary data—Data collected from personal interviews, completed questionnaires, surveys, direct information or observations and experiments are known as primary data. Primary data for this research were the information collected through the fieldwork from the organisations and interviewees.

3.3.2 Secondary data—When previously collected primary data stored in different types of memories and documents these become secondary data. Some books related to demography and culture of South Asian ethnic minorities in the UK, the practice of domestic violence against women and different types of research reports on forced marriage in the UK were the major secondary sources of data for this study. Publications of FMU and other organisations dealing with forced marriage, Internet resources: particularly the web pages of FMU and other related organisations also were the sources of secondary data for this research.

3.4 Methods of Data Collection

There was an extensive literature review of published national and local documents relating to forced marriage. The main purpose of the literature review was to collate the information available on the profile of victims, the circumstances of forced marriage and the types and availability of social work support from different agencies. It played the most important role to find out the organisations who deal with forced marriage and the key people or professionals in the community working with forced marriage cases. Based on that information following methods were employed:

3.4.1 Survey

A mapping survey was conducted over 8 national, regional and local organisations that are working to tackle forced marriage to a range of communities including British Bangladeshi community especially across London and Birmingham. The questionnaire asked about socio-demographic profile of victims and service responses. The questionnaire focused on the nature and types of available social work services and their effectiveness.

There were several important reasons to choose survey as a method for this research. Surveys gather data about relationships between people, places and things as they exist in the real world setting. Those relationships cannot all be examined in laboratory experiments. Moreover, surveys allow the collection of data about what people think and feel and facilitate the collection of information in great breadth and depth. Surveys are also very cost-efficient.

3.4.2 Interviews

i) Familiarisation interviews with 6 individuals purposively selected from different social backgrounds e.g., people from generation I, II, III, professionals, home makers, community guardians, community volunteers, students, etc. The purpose of such interviews was to have some introductory but practical perceptions about forced marriage and the support services.

ii) Interviews with 6 stakeholders that include people such as support workers, health professionals, teachers, immigration advisers, religious leaders or Imams, etc. These interviews were conducted to understand the responses of service providers and victims on forced marriage. Their insight and experience built up a confidence to answer the research question.

iii) In-depth interviews with 2 survivors of forced marriage with an average length of one hour. Survivors are those who have passed the incidents and now living their new life by ending that forced marriage. Their statements covered the causes of the incidents to effectiveness and limitations of the social work services. A number of survivors were identified through snowball sampling by stakeholders and the agencies. From that list 2 survivors were interviewed purposively.

This method was used to collect qualitative data by setting up a situation (the interview) that allows a respondent the time and scope to talk about their opinions on a particular subject. The focus of the interviews were decided by the researcher and there were areas the researcher was interested in exploring. The objective was to understand the respondents' point of view rather than making generalisations about behaviour. It is relatively easy to use this method with a representative sample although this method takes time and effort (since an in-depth interview takes time and demands the interviewing skills of the interviewer/researcher).

3.5 Techniques of Data Collection

To survey the organisations pre-tested questionnaires including open-ended, semi-closed and closed questions written in English language were used. In the survey, researcher used a combination of self-administered (distributed by himself and then collected the filled up questionnaires) and e-mail questionnaires (sent and received the filled up questionnaires by Internet mail). [*See appendix 1*]

To interview the respondents, pre-tested semi-structured topic guidelines used to get the answers of research questions. There were three different types of guidelines with little differences to conduct three different types of interviews: Familiarisation interviews, interviews with Stakeholders and In-depth interviews with survivors. [*See appendices 2-5*]

3.6 Methods of Analysis

As statistics is a symphony based on two notes: means and standard deviations, qualitative data analysis is a symphony based on three notes: **noticing, collecting, and thinking** about interesting things. That is why all interviews were analysed manually. First of all, sorting, coding and sifting made sense in analysis. Then bracketing, phenomenological reduction and extracting general and unique themes from all the interviews made a composite summary. As there were small portion of statistical data the knowledge of means and standard deviations used manually rather than any software package like SPSS or MINITAB. Overall, data manipulation, classification, tabulation and largely the judgement were relevant to analyse the data. Finally, the variety of methods used provided a degree of triangulation, and also enough breadth to allow general patterns to emerge.

3.7 Ethical Issues

In general, ethics is norms for conduct that distinguish between acceptable and unacceptable behaviour. In this research, it is a perspective for deciding how to act and analyse complex problems and issues like culture, ethnicity, minority, religion, professional code of conduct etc.

The biggest challenge in this study was that existing knowledge around forced marriage is largely centred on South Asian and Muslim communities. This could lead to an assumption that these communities are especially vulnerable to this issue. So it was necessary to clarify some important considerations to contextualise the higher number of cases within these communities. These include demographics, as South Asian communities are the largest ethnic minority group in the UK. In addition, there have historically been very articulate and powerful South Asian feminist groups that have challenged gender related issues within these communities, including forced marriage, honour related violence and dowry related violence. For these reasons, there have also been many studies on forms of marriage within South Asian communities, including arranged marriages that are sometimes confused with forced marriages (Caroll, 1998; Gangoli et al., 2006).

At the same time as an insider in the community, researcher (the author) had to keep in mind the cultural settings during data collection. Studies showed that the maximum forced marriages are practising over women. So that some women based organisations along with women respondents came across the study and some of them refused to talk because of gender differences with the researcher (as a male person). Another sensitive issue was the religion here. In a Muslim community and which was also an ethnic minority with traditional conservative philosophy, the researcher, as a man from the same community and religion experienced difficulties in discussing the topics such as 'sexuality or sexual orientation', 'love marriage and arranged marriage', etc. Therefore, the strategy adopted by the researcher was to ensure that ethnicity and gender would overcome any potential resistance there might have been to speaking openly or critically about forced marriage.

Above all, protection of participants through the informed consent process favours formalised interaction between researcher and participants. So the researcher was always honest about who is he, what his research is about, why he wants to talk, and what he will do with the information. Before interviewing the respondents, they were informed about the project through a kind of information letter and were invited to take part. Then only after getting positive responses interviews were conducted. They had the right of withdrawal from the participation during interview and even after data collection.

While interviewing survivors of forced marriage, researcher was very careful about the values such as fairness, autonomy, integrity and results that formed a supportive framework of interviewing survivors. It was helpful to built up a rapport before the interviewing day. He also gave time after interviews to support them emotionally to remove their uneasiness and depression. It was a good idea not to ask any direct question from the guidelines to interview. Researcher was listening like a story and pointed the queries as a concept from previous studies rather than interrogating that made survivors easy to answer.

Furthermore, throughout data collection, analysis, report writing and now in publication the author has focused on the following factors—

Confidentiality: Protect confidential communications, such as questionnaire, interview scripts, and records.

Human Subjects Protection: When conducting research on forced marriage, the researcher tried to minimise harms and risks. He has maximised benefits and took special precautions with vulnerable respondents. He has the respect for human dignity, privacy, and autonomy.

Honesty: Researcher did not fabricate, falsify or misrepresent data.

Objectivity: Avoided bias in research design, data analysis, data interpretation and other aspects of research where objectivity was expected or required. Researcher tried not to disclose personal interests that could affect research.

Legality: Researcher knew and obeyed relevant laws and institutional and governmental policies on researching such issues.

3.8 Limitations of the Research

Researching on any subject is undoubtedly complex. The researcher was acutely aware that the study might have been perceived as intrusion into cultural practices and that perception might have impacted on the responses made in the interviews. Access to all the resources and respondents was difficult for the researcher. Above all, this research has some limitations during data collection and analysis. If highlighted some points of limitations these could be as following:

➢ Surveys have a number of limitations. In this research, the most serious weakness concerns the validity and reliability of responses obtained to questions.

➢ In purposive sampling, researcher chose who he likes (within defined criteria) and might therefore select those who were easiest to interview, so bias can result. The disadvantage with snowballing is that a sampling frame created using this method alone might be prone to bias. This is because those who know each other might have similar behaviours and attitudes or might influence each other in relation to the research. Those that are missed may had quite different characteristics.

➢ In interviewing, the weakness is largely depends on the skill of the interviewers (the ability to think of questions during the interview, for example) and articulacy of respondents. However, as a beginner, researcher was dependent on the answers of the respondents. The researcher had no real ways of knowing about how truthful the responses were. Respondents might not consciously lie but might have imperfect recall. As some questions were being asked to remember things that happened weeks, months or years ago it is likely that they would actually remember very little about what happened.

➢ It was noticed that respondents including the organisations were unable to answer few questions accurately or they missed the main points of those questions especially in survey.

➢ Finally, analysing qualitative data in this research was essentially a simple process of coding, sorting and sifting of facts, so it might misguide the researcher from the main theme. A qualitative researcher known as Wiseman (1979:278) said that the totality of philosophy as expressed by the interviewees, which is closely related to the major goal of the study, may destroy by breaking down data into its constituent parts and also can mislead the analyst. Although to minimise this problem, after sorting and coding researcher heard the recording and read the transcripts again to find out any missing or misdirection in the collection that differs from interview conversations.

Chapter 4

Results

4.1 Findings from the Survey

Survey questionnaires were divided into parts to know about circumstances of forced marriage, existing social work services and the evaluation of social work services. Following are the data divided into three major parts as collected through original questionnaires.

4.1.1 Circumstances of Forced Marriage

4.1.1.1 Maximum Practice of Forced Marriage

To know who shows the maximum practice of forced marriage a group of south Asian ethnic minorities were listed to identify by the organisations.

Table 1: Maximum practice of forced marriage

Ethnic group	N	%
Pakistanis	7	87.5
Bangladeshis	1	12.5
Indians	0	0
Others	0	0
Total	8	100

The result shows that majority organisations (87.5%) identified Pakistani community as one who shows the maximum practice of forced marriage. On the other hand, a small number of organisations (12.5%) listed Bangladeshi community among all south Asian ethnic minority groups living in the UK.

4.1.1.2 British Bangladeshi Victims

Some organisations said that they do not keep any particular statistics about the number of victims from different communities. But from their experience they shared the following data.

Table 2: British Bangladeshi victims

British Bangladeshi Victims	N	%
5-10%	2	25
11-15%	0	0
16-20%	4	50
21-25%	2	25
More than 25%	0	0
Total	8	100

The result says that most of the organisations (25%+50%=75%) found not more than 20% victims of forced marriage is from British Bangladeshi community. On the other hand, a quarter of total organisations (25%) showed that about 21-25% of total victims is from this community.

4.1.1.3 Age of Majority Victims

To determine the age of majority victims, a list of average age ranges were presented to the organisations.

Table 3: Age of majority victims

Age Ranges	N	%
From 13-17 years old	2	25
From 18-22 Years old	6	75
From 23-27 years old	0	0
Other	0	0
Total	8	100

It is clear from the table, three quarter of total organisations (75%) told that the highest number of victims is from the age of 18-22 years. Where a quarter of total organisations (25%) claimed that there is high number of victims from the age of 13-17 years.

4.1.1.4 Rise or Decline in the Number of Cases

To see whether the organisations are receiving more or less complaints of forced marriage this year (2010) than last year (2009), a question was raised.

Table 4: Rise or decline in the number of cases

Number of cases this year (2010)	N	%
More	5	62.5
Less	3	37.5
Total	8	100

The table shows around two third of total organisations (62.5%) said that there are more cases reported this year in comparison to last year. On the other hand, more than one third organisations (37.5%) claimed that there is a decline in the complaints of forced marriage this year.

4.1.1.5 Main Reasons behind Forced Marriage

The following table discovers the main reasons behind forced marriage. Organisations were asked to select three answers including an open ended choice.

Table 5: Reasons behind forced marriage (N=24)

Main reasons	N	%
Long standing family commitments and preserving family honour	7	29.17
Assisting claims for UK residence and citizenship	7	29.17
Achieving financial gain	3	12.5
Ensuring land, property and wealth remain within the family	4	16.66

Others:
  i) Controlling unwanted behaviour and sexuality (more specifically women)
  ii) Homophobia
  iii) Preventing relationships outside the ethnic, cultural, religious or caste groups
	3	12.5

Total	24	100

(**Note:** Three answers were taken from each organisation as a result 24 answers were found from 8 organisations. Percentage has been calculated on the basis of that number.)

The result shows that around one third of total organisations (29.17%) supported long standing family commitments and preserving family honour as one of the main reasons behind forced marriage. Another same number claimed that assisting claims for UK residence and citizenship is also a major reason behind forced marriage. Some organisations (12.5%) discovered controlling unwanted behaviour and sexuality, homophobia and preventing unsuitable relationships as the main reasons behind forced marriage.

4.1.2 Existing Social Work Services

4.1.2.1 Groups Served by the Organisations

To specify the groups supported by the organisations in response to forced marriage following table is constructed. Organisations selected all groups they serve from the questionnaires. Multiple answers found from each organisation.

Table 6: Client groups (N=23)

Client Groups	N	%
Adult female	3	13.05
Adult male	1	4.35
Both of adult male and female	4	17.39
Children	7	30.44
Disable	2	8.69
Some one from LGBT community	2	8.69
Other voluntary organisations	4	17.39
Total	23	100

The table says that around one third of organisations (30.44%) pointed children as a priority group in response to forced marriage. Both of adult male and female are the second largest group of priority (17.39%) as it contains female victims. Because there are organisations (13.05%) who only serve female victims. A very small number of organisations (4.35%) serve adult male victims only. Someone from LGBT community is the main focus of some organisations (8.69%) also.

4.1.2.2 The Route of Getting Clients

The following table shows how the victims come into contact with relevant organisations. Organisations had the choice to choose multiple answers.

Table 7: Route of getting clients (N=20)

Route of getting clients	N	%
Referred by FMU	6	30
Referred by educational institutions	2	10
Referred by any other professionals	2	10
Clients come directly through media (internet, newspaper, magazine, social journal, billboards, etc.)	6	30
Referred by clients' friends	2	10
Other	2	10
Total	20	100

Interestingly, the result shows around one third of total victims (30%) go to the organisations through FMU. But it is also true that another one third of total victims go to the organisations by themselves through the knowledge of media. A small number (10%) either go to the organisations through referral of any other professionals or educational institutions or by clients' friends.

4.1.2.3 Types of Services

This section provides information about services available in different organisations for the victims and survivors of forced marriage. Organisations chose multiple answers as they provide more than one services.

Table 8: Support services (N=28)

Services	N	%
Information and Advice	7	25
Advocacy and Counselling	7	25
Legal advice and Representations	4	14.28
Refuge	4	14.28
Other: i) Social support group/ One to one support ii) Sexual health screenings and testing iii) Referral and networking iv) Youth project v) Outreach programme vi) Self-help support services in different languages vii) Personal telephone support	6	21.44
Total	28	100

The table shows that a quarter of total organisations (25%) provide information and advice to the victims and survivors of forced marriage. Another quarter of total organisations (25%) provide advocacy and counselling. Some organisations (14.28%) provide the most important service—refuge for the victims.

4.1.2.4 Preventive Activities

This section describes what sort of preventive activities are initiated by the organisations to minimise forced marriage in the community.

Table 9: Preventive activities (N=20)

Preventive activities	N	%
Educating teachers, community workers, health professionals and all other relevant personnel about the issues surrounding forced marriage and the presenting symptoms	2	10
Circulating and displaying relevant information	5	25
Sticker, leaflets, billboards etc. on important places including train/ bus stations and all other public transports	1	5
Involve young people by arranging workshops about forced marriage	6	30

Other:
  i) inform the Muslim community through religious advice about the unacceptability of forced marriage in Islam
  ii) Extensive use of all forms of media working with local community organisations
  iii) Campaign programmes
	6	30

Total	20	100

The result shows among all the preventive activities initiated by the organisations, around one third (30%) is the extensive use of all forms of media, working with local community organisations, campaign programmes, etc. Again, another one third (30%) responded that involve young people by arranging workshops about forced marriage. Sticker, leaflets, billboards etc. on important places including train and bus stations and all other public transports is the lowest number (5%) of total activities initiated by the organisations.

4.1.3 Evaluation of Services

4.1.3.1 Number of Staff Working

The table discovers number of staff working in each organisation to deal with forced marriage cases.

Table 10: Number of staff working

Number of staff	N	%
1-10	2	25
11-20	3	37.5
More than 20	3	37.5
Total	8	100

The table says that more than one third of total organisations (37.5%) have more than 20 staff who deal with forced marriage cases. Again, a quarter of total organisations (25%) have 1 to 10 staff to work with the victims.

4.1.3.2 Gender of Support Workers

As there are male and female victims of forced marriage an attempt has been made to know whether the organisations have both of male and female support workers or not.

Table 11: Gender of support workers

Male and female workers	N	%
Yes	5	62.5
No	3	37.5
Total	8	100

The result says around two third of total organisations (62.5%) have both of male and female support workers to deal with forced marriage cases. More than one third of total organisations (37.5%) are working with either male or female workers only.

4.1.3.3 Gaps in Existing Services

Organisations were asked to choose multiple answers about the gaps they find in existing services.

Table 12: Gaps in existing services (N=25)

Gaps	N	%
Support with getting legal services	3	12
Victims with 'No recourse to public funds' have restrictions in access	3	12
Support with housing, school, self esteem issues	7	28
Lack of faith with support services and criminal justice	2	8
Lack of Asian advocates	3	12
Others: i) Priorities are not given within affected communities ii) Lack of awareness amongst victims of what help is available iii) Fear from many educational establishments of being culturally insensitive and fear of 'upsetting' school governors by displayingg leaflets on their premises about the subject	7	28
Total	25	100

The table shows that support with housing, school, self esteem issues are reported highly (28%) as a gap. At the same time, other gaps including priorities are not given within affected communities, lack of awareness amongst victims of what help is available, fear from many educational establishments of being culturally insensitive and fear of 'upsetting' school governors by displaying leaflets on their premises about the subject etc. are identified by the organisations as major gaps. Lack of faith with support services and criminal justice were other gaps identified by some of the organisations (8%).

4.1.3.4 Recommendations

At the end of the questionnaire, organisations were asked to give some recommendations to improve the communication to support the victims of forced marriage.

Table 13: Recommendations (N=25)

Recommendations	N	%
TV campaigns	5	20
Radio including Asian networks	2	8
Information at places of worship/ Involve religious leaders	7	28
Schools and colleges can introduce forced marriage into the curriculum of relevant classes by discussing different types of marriage	7	28
Others: i) Work in grass-roots level with community organisations ii) Placing leaflets in places of public use, i.e., GP surgeries, hospitals. iii) Advertisements on public transport.	4	16
Total	25	100

The above table shows that more than a quarter of organisations (28%) recommended about schools and colleges who can introduce forced marriage into the curriculum of relevant classes by discussing different types of marriage and their affect. Again, providing information at places of worship and involve religious leaders were focused by the same number of organisations. Some organisations (8%) were also recommended about the improvement of communication by radio including Asian networks.

4.2 Findings from the Interviews

To present the data obtained from interviews sub sections have been used in this section on the basis of related questions asked to different groups of people with some direct quotations from the transcripts. This ensures that no original data will be missing in this chapter of data presentation.

4.2.1 Definition of Forced Marriage

As it is a study on forced marriage, a basic query was about respondents' general understanding of forced marriage. From their answers some words came out about forced marriage such as 'cheating by parents', 'planning of marriage without permission', 'consent is not voluntarily given', 'marriage against their wish', 'not chosen by bride and/or bridegroom', etc. These words simply make an answer that forced marriage is a marriage against the will or wish where consent is not taken from the girl and/or boy. They are not agreeing with and have not given their consent voluntarily to marry.

> *"Some one being asked to marry not because he or she chooses but has been chosen by others."*
> —A Social Worker, working with children

4.2.2 Difference between Forced Marriage and Arranged Marriage

To differentiate forced marriage from those known as arranged marriage most of the respondents said that arranged marriage and forced marriage are two different things. Arranged marriage is where two individuals are brought together, introduced, as two individuals having the opportunity to talk with each other and decide whether marry or not. But in forced marriage they have no opportunity to talk and to decide. In arranged marriages, most of the time family or parents (mainly fathers) choose first then children get the opportunity to choose and then both of intending spouses along with their families make decision. Where in forced marriages, family or parents (mainly fathers) choose and decide without talking to their children. Few people strongly raised the situation of brides by saying that they have less opportunity to choose or decide than bridegrooms.

4.2.3 Arranged Marriage Disappearing or Changing?

Arranged marriage is not forced marriage but in some cases it can be seen that parents are trying to arrange a marriage—they are giving options to choose but children are not cooperating. May be because of love affairs or for some other reasons they do not want to choose from the list of their parents. As a result, the concept of arranged marriage is either disappearing or changing some how. On this topic, interviewees tried to show the patterns of traditional and modern arranged marriages. They said that the concept of arrange marriage is not disappearing but the arrangement is changing. Where earlier all the time parents or family used to find a proposal for their children now sometimes both bride and bridegroom choose first then seek permission of their parents. Earlier there were some arranged marriages which used to fix without seeing each other on parents' decision and the parties accepted cordially as it was common to their culture. But now this trend is disappearing. The traditional pattern of arranged marriage is changed and it is gaining modern trends rather than disappearing. That indicates that there was the tradition of arranged marriage, it is now and might be present in the future.

"Arrange marriage is declining... Parents are giving
some idealistic choices with some boundaries that
selected person should be from same background,
denomination, same religion, same caste,
same language speaking... Parents are giving room
but narrowing the options."
—A Health Trainer, working in Tower Hamlets

When most of the respondents think the arranged marriage is not disappearing but the patterns are changing day by day, few people think it is declining because of the authority of parents where they set out boundaries to choose from.

4.2.4 Factors Affect Forced Marriage

Experts think religion, culture, education, social class and other factors like these can affect the arrangement of forced marriage. To answer these questions all of the respondents agreed that culture of any particular community where they have traditional superstitions, bad customs, certain beliefs causes forced marriage. And these are closely related with social class, caste, and lineage of the families involved. To remove those things from the culture, education can play the most important role. So education can affect the arrangement of forced marriage. Again, majority respondents said that religion has no affect in the arrangement of forced marriage but it is the culture of misunderstanding religion that is traditionally present in some communities. People misinterpret the religion or they have lack of knowledge about religion. For example, Islam does not support a marriage where either the man or woman is unhappy with the set up. But some Muslims use their power of authority and cultural misunderstanding to arrange such forced marriages and then hide behind the religion of Islam to justify their actions. On the other hand, few respondents clearly addressed religion as a factor in forced marriage.

"Religion stops to be a homosexual or bisexual so
religion is responsible in some cases
to force into marriage."
—A Support Worker, working with Gay
and Bisexual Asian men

Religion of Islam prohibits homosexuality as a result indirectly has a role in forcing some one to marry from opposite sex. On this topic few respondents including an Imam said that marriage depends on both of the partners rather than their parents or family. Islam said not to intervene on others' personal life. Forced marriage is totally prohibited in Islam but it is happening within Muslim communities because of their tradition and lack of knowledge. Islam does not prohibit any act without proper direction for solution. And force in anything could not be a solution.

> *"Blaming religion is the easiest thing though they find their own prospective in that. It's true that Islam does not allow same sex marriages and partnerships so you may treat that particular person in Islamic perspective if he or she is a Muslim. Religion says to teach about the danger of homosexuality not to force into marry."*
> —An Imam, working in a mosque

4.2.5 Causes behind Forced Marriage

This part is about respondents' common perception regarding the causes behind forced marriage. All of the respondents mentioned some common reasons of forced marriage. They are: assisting relatives to come in the UK, family commitments and relation build up within lineage, financial gain, homophobia, social status and tribe, name and fame of that family back home etc. Some respondents also added that parents been uneducated in the sense of their religious requirements so they failed to recognise their true responsibility towards children. Again few people think it is parents' love for their children's well-being.

> *"They forced me just to keep their commitment made years ago . . . they do care their honour . . . they do not care about their own daughter."*
> —Sharmin[5], a survivor

Interestingly, someone, who is working as an immigration adviser, thinks there is only one reason behind forced marriage and it is border-crossing.

"Border-crossing is in the root of some problems. Border divides countries . . . people from third world countries, who live under poverty line, want to come to first world always. Earlier, people came here in the first world by selling their property and sacrificing their relations so they have an underlying commitment to help those who are in the third world. As a result, they force their children to marry someone from back home. If there is no border or boundary there would be no Visa or Immigration things to encourage such marriages."
—An Immigration Adviser,
who was working in Sylhet, Bangladesh

4.2.6 Existing Social Work Services

In response to the question regarding the services available for the victims of forced marriage all most all the people who are not working directly with domestic violence or forced marriage said that they have no idea about the existing services for the victims if there is any. Some of them said that they just know it is against the law of the country so police can help the victims. It can be brought to the court for justice under human rights. If outside the UK, the British High commission may help the victims.

"I had no idea where to go and how . . . I thought there must be a way . . . I just wanted to inform the British High Commission."
—Anamika[6], a survivor

On the other hand, the people who are directly dealing with forced marriage cases or any other domestic violence boldly mentioned the most common services for the victims. They are: giving information and advice, referral to relevant organisations, specialised counselling and refuge. Some of them also listed other services such as support the victims under social support groups, one to one support, sexual health screenings and testing, self-help support services in several community languages etc. Few of them added that there are also some special support programmes such as workshops, youth projects, outreach programmes etc.

> *"We offer counselling, sexual health screenings and testing, social support group. Asian gay and bi-sexual may feel isolated in the community so they can talk and share with people having same problem here. We do refer for refuge or other services such as immigration advice, employment or any other help to relevant organisations."*
> —A Support Worker, working with Gay
> and Bisexual Asian men

4.2.7 Gaps in Support Services

The existing support services in the public, private and voluntary sectors are not adequate in dealing with forced marriage cases means there are some gaps. Majority respondents mentioned some common gaps in the available support services. Services are not multi-cultural or religious. They are serving either on the basis of specific religion or culture. But culture and religion are different in terms of practice for all the communities where forced marriage is a problem. For example, mixed refuge is not appropriate. Again, most of the respondents made clear that more Asian people from all affected communities with adequate qualification should be engaged in studying forced marriage and to support victims as well. This is because an insider can understand better and introduce effective working strategies. On the other hand, they can speak the languages of victims and understand the limitations and feelings. They think FMU along with charity organisations are not funding or implementing programmes effectively to abolish forced marriage.

> *"I do not see any notable project funded by FMU that any reputable organisation can take on to educate people, to enlighten the community, parents and young people."*
> —A Health Professional,
> working in a community organisation

Few respondents highlighted that when they consider support for the victims from LGBT community it becomes more complex to serve. First of all, the organisations are not well-equipped and well-funded for those victims. Again, it is hard to support those victims along with his or her family.

4.2.8 People with 'No Recourse to Public Funds' (NRPF)

People, who have NRPF, are likely to have a restriction on receiving public funds. It mainly includes income support and housing benefit with some other social services. If someone with NRPF becomes the victim of forced marriage or any other domestic violence it causes serious suffering. On those circumstances, government or charity organisations can take initiatives to help them. Few responses were too different where respondents said that UK government can support them though victims' government is responsible for them. Because when they enter here with NRPF status they knew that they will not have such facilities and they will be able to support them in any situation. But majority respondents replied that UK government should think about them because it is happening inside the UK. Victims should have access to the services. In such cases, Local Authorities have to ensure that victims are getting facilities regardless of their immigration status.

> *"Refuge should be free of cost. It is UK government's responsibility to ensure that victim is getting support regardless of immigration status like NRPF."*
> —A Community Volunteer, working in London

The professionals directly dealing with forced marriage said that only for the people on temporary and settlement visa, have NRPF for first two years. In these two years immigrants have difficulty in getting social services but still there are free refuges and charity organisations that can help. Southall Black Sisters introduced 'No Recourse Fund' to support them. Stonewall Housing and Albert Kennedy Trust provide LGBT refuge and those are free of cost for certain periods. Later, people who have ILR can access to housing benefit and income support.

4.2.9 Tackling Forced Marriage

This section describes those who in the community should be involved as the community has a role in tackling forced marriage. Almost all of the respondents said that the whole community should work together. Local councils along with educational and religious institutions such as Mosques should educate the community and that is the key to abolish forced marriage. But victims should look for the services so that they can get help. Parents and community guardians usually elders in the community can make a difference rather than specific organisations or professionals.

One interesting response was about government. The government should take strict steps to stop forced marriage if it is really a big problem.

> *"Government—the last organisation that we made, that we arranged to support us, to ensure our safety and protection. That's why we live under a government, isn't it?"*
> —Former Immigration Adviser, lives in London

4.2.10 Government's Effectiveness

Although government initiated some support programmes and enacted laws regarding forced marriage majority of the respondents agreed that government is poor in communicating message about forced marriage. At the same time, few strongly disagreed by saying that UK government is good enough and quite successful in compared to all other governments in the world regarding this issue.

> *"I was totally unfamiliar with the organisations including Forced Marriage Unit . . . I might have heard about them earlier."*
> —A Survivor, living in Birmingham

4.2.11 Recommendations to Improve the Services

Respondents who identified gaps in existing services and raising community awareness were asked to recommend how to improve the services and communication. Lots of recommendations came out from the interviews. Government should educate public about the danger of forced marriage. National Curriculum can introduce the concept of forced marriage under the course of citizenship. Organisations need publicity that they deal with forced marriage. They need outreach work in community settings; mosques, schools and so on. Domestic violence units are working but better to involve local community organisations who are working for the benefit of the community.

> *"You need the whole community not only people from the government body or academics, you need to get grassroots people as well."*
> —A Father, an automotive engineer in Birmingham

> *"More grassroots level funding and more grassroots level initiatives to work within the community may be by recruiting people from the community and to create innovative methods to prevent forced marriage."*
> —A Support Worker, working in London

4.2.12 Life of the Survivors Responded in this Study

In this part, some questions about survivors' basic information and story of incidents are focused which were not covered by the above sections. Both of the survivors were from Bangladeshi community and Muslim female. They were forced into marry in the age of 20 and 33 respectively.

Survivor 1

Anamika (not true name) was in a professional training in London. She was sent to Bangladesh by her family on a lie that her mother is ill. After her arrival she was imprisoned at home. They took away all her documents and bank cards. She thinks that they forced her as she was aged and not wanted to marry at that moment because of her professional career. She also believes that her family did not like her love affair and they also wanted to have some one from equal family. However, a local NGO working for women's rights in Bangladesh helped to process a case in the court with the support of some of her friends living in the UK. Finally, she was free to come back to UK by ending that marriage in Bangladesh. British High Commission in Bangladesh played an important role for her safety once the case came to attention.

> *"I requested the court not to put my parents in trouble because of what they have done. I love my family."*
> —Anamika, a survivor from London

At the moment, she does not have good relationship with her family but still she loves and misses them. However, she is married to her boyfriend and living happily in the UK.

Survivor 2

Sharmin (not real name), who finished her GCSEs few years ago, went to Bangladesh for a family holiday. After a week her father said that her marriage is fixed with her cousin (son of her father's sister). Her mother explained that they have promised her aunt a long time ago about this marriage. Later she discovered her elder brother (with whom she had a friendly relation) already hide her passport. As a result, she had no options but to marry her cousin. She was under strict supervision of her father and brother even after returning to the UK. She could not go out alone. At this situation she was crying all the time. Luckily her mother was always supporting her emotionally. Finally, she refused to apply in bringing her husband here to the UK and her father tortured her physically. Somehow (she did not want to mention) police came across the incident and local domestic violence team helped her to get divorce and managed refuge for her. At the moment she is living by herself at her own home and has good relationship with her mother. She thinks that now she is happy.

*"When it happened, I felt I am lost some where in a
deep and dark forest . . . all alone . . . Now it's like I am
living my own life where I can make decisions
of every single thing."*
—Sharmin, a survivor from Birmingham

4.2.13 Comments about the Research

As a final comment, most of the respondents appreciated the study especially all who responded in familiarisation interviews. They said that it is a wonderful way to engage and educate people about forced marriage. The report can be presented as a book in near future.

*"The research is successful as it is creating awareness at
least among respondents like me."*
—A Mother, lives in Birmingham

*"After getting your report do a small event within the
East London area to kind of publicise or inform the
community about your findings based upon research.
It could be an asset to the community. Once you get
your degree, bring the organisations you come across to
arrange an event and show people how important it is!"*
—A Community Worker, working in East London

---

[5] **Sharmin is not the real name of the respondent**
[6] **Anamika is not the real name of the respondent**

Chapter 5

Discussion

This chapter covers the discussion of the data presented in earlier chapter. The discussion of the findings relates the study to the context and theoretical framework drawn in the literature review chapter.

5.1 Circumstances of Forced Marriage

5.1.1 Cultural Issues in Forced Marriage

Forced marriage is that marriage where one or both of people who are getting married do not give their full and free consent. These marriages are arranged by the parents, family or other people rather than the intending spouses. But this is not same as the arranged marriage. In arranged marriage, someone else may choose but both of intending spouses decide whether to enter into marriage or not. Historically, arranged marriages are always a common phenomenon in South Asian communities. Arranged marriages are seen as diminishing the likelihood of divorce because the partners are chosen for their compatibility and from suitable family backgrounds. On the basis of this logic those communities, especially Bangladeshi community prefers marriages to be arranged by families within the clan or extended family and love marriages are not the most appropriate way of finding a life-partner. Whatever, forced marriage was present in those communities; still it is there along with arranged marriage. The patterns of arranged marriage are changing day by day. Nowadays, parents or family also accepting the choice of their children on some circumstances where earlier only parents or family used to choose and then children agreed to marry. However, still daughters and sisters are not getting priorities to choose their mates in arranged marriages because of the patriarchal nature of the society. On the other hand, in forced marriage, neither a boy nor a girl has any right to talk about their own marriage. Culture, in the sense of traditional superstitions and bad customs, can influence the arrangement of forced marriage. And these are interrelated with social class, caste, and lineage of the concerned families. To remove these things from the culture, community education can be helpful. Furthermore, misuse of religious feelings largely encouraging forced marriage.

Even after lots of works to abolish forced marriage the record showed most of the organisations find more cases are reporting than previous years. Front-line practitioners and support workers think that it is because of the awareness build up against the practice. People are becoming more aware of their rights and choices, they are logging their complaints. The practitioners think people are reporting the incidents more than earlier but the actual number of incidents should be lower at the moment. However, study found that maximum practice of forced marriage is visible in Pakistani community while Bangladeshi community is in the second position among all south Asian ethnic minorities living in the UK. Again, according to the statistics of the majority organisations, the number of British Bangladeshi victims is not more than one fifth (20%) of total victims. Most of the victims of forced marriage are from the age of 18-22 years found in this study. But the data also showed any one of any age can be forced into marriage as one survivor interviewed was forced in her age of 33.

5.1.2 Causes behind Forced Marriage

The study found lots of causes behind forced marriage. The following are the major ones:

i) Long standing family commitments and traditional mind set,
ii) Assisting relatives to claim for UK residence and citizenship,

iii) Stronger relation build up within same family (*Ghusti*), kinship ties (*Khandhan*), caste or caste-like groups (*Zat*) and clan (*Bongsho*),

iv) Ensuring land, property and wealth remain within the family and achieving financial gain,

v) Homophobia, controlling unwanted behaviour and sexuality (more specifically applied to women),

vi) Preventing relationships outside the ethnic, cultural, religious and caste groups,

vii) To stop love affairs and sex before marriage,

viii) Parents been uneducated about true responsibility towards children (in the sense of their religious requirements and obligations),

ix) Parents' blind love for their children's well-being,

x) Attractiveness and non-attractiveness of bride and bridegroom (more specifically applied to women).

Although their religion (Islam) prohibits forced marriage the ignorance about religion and lack of knowledge about parenting (guided by the religion) made an environment where any outsider can blame the religion easily. At the same time, homosexuality or bisexuality can be seen as an emerging reason behind forced marriage. And Islam strictly prohibits it (Al Qur'an, 4:15-16; 7:80-81). In this point, it should be noted that Islam does not suggest forced marriage as a solution to homosexuality and bisexuality. Islamic 'Nikah' (marriage) cannot be completed if both parties do not give their consent by saying 'Qabul' (I agree). So if someone is homosexual than she or he will not give her or his consent to marry someone from opposite sex. As a result, it can be said that Muslims are not allowed to force someone into marriage even if the person is homosexual. The religion also reminds Muslims not to interfere in others' rights including their mothers' and sisters' rights (Hadith Muslim 4257; recorded by Mughirah B. Shuba). The parents or the Muslim community have a responsibility to ensure that children are getting appropriate education and training to avoid being an offender defined under Islamic law and order which are based on humanity and mankind for the well-being of the world.

5.2 Existing Social Work Services

5.2.1 Available Services for the Victims and Survivors

There are lots of support services available for the victims and survivors of forced marriage. Among those services the most common one provided by all the organisations is information and advice. The next one is advocacy and counselling. At the same time, some organisations (14.28%) are giving refuge to the victims of forced marriage. And most of them are for women and children. However, the study identified the major services below:

i)   Information and Advice,
ii)   Advocacy and Counselling,
iii)   Legal Advice and Representations,
iv)   Refuge,
v)   Social Support Group,
vi)   One to One Support,
vii)   Sexual Health Screenings and Testing,
viii) Referral and Networking between Organisations,
ix)   Youth Projects,
x)   Outreach Programmes,
xi)   Self-help Support Services in different Languages,
xii)   Personal Telephone Support.

Most of these services are appropriate for all types of victims of forced marriage. Although there are few services designed to help the survivors of forced marriage only. Supporting individual clients over telephone as and when they feel they need to talk to someone is very useful service for the survivors. An organisation said that their oldest supported client has been on their books for 10 years and still contacts them most weeks for support. Few organisations reported that their support staff is always on call to provide support to the survivors. They offer all kinds of guidance and support when and where needed. It starts from placing them into their own houses rather than refuge. Their main priority is to move those victims to live their life by their own, free of oppression and abuse, and love whomever they choose. In short, specialist counselling services, housing, education and advice are core to support the survivors of forced marriage.

5.2.2 Preventive Activities for Potential Victims

The study found some common preventive activities initiated by the voluntary and charity organisations dealing with forced marriage and all other domestic violence to help the potential victims. Below are the major ones:

i) Involve young people by arranging workshops about forced marriage,
ii) Campaign programmes,
iii) Educating teachers, community workers, health professionals and all other relevant personnel about the issues surrounding forced marriage and the presenting symptoms,
iv) Use of all forms of media,
v) Circulating and displaying relevant information,
vi) inform the Muslim community through religious advice about the unacceptability of forced marriage in Islam,
vii) Sticker, leaflets, billboards etc. on important places including train and bus stations and all other public transports,
viii) Working with local community organisations to work from within the community.

Within all of these preventive activities, the most common ones practised by almost all of the organisations are to involve young people by arranging workshops, use of all forms of media and campaign programmes. There are also some special support programmes initiated by few organisations such as one to one outreach service through regular outreach sessions. These include crisis and short term counselling, dealing with family conflict, coping mechanisms, advice on health care, education, employment, advice and information on housing options, accessing more specialist advice and information. Again, in campaign, there are several ways to raise the awareness, for instances, Real Man Campaign, Empowering Women Awards, Campaign through Movies and Songs, Expect Respect Campaign, The Body Shop Campaign, Award Wining Celebrity Campaign and so on.

5.3 Evaluation of Social Work Services

5.3.1 Success

As women and children are the vast majority of victims, organisations are mainly focusing on them. Children and women are in the main attention of one third organisations (30.44%). There are some organisations (13.05%) dealing with women victims only as women are the most vulnerable group. Again, some organisations (17.39%) work with both male and female victims. From this statistics, it can be easily identified that women and children are getting priority in response to forced marriage. On the other hand, majority clients either come through referral of FMU or directly through help of internet or printing media by their own (30% and 30% respectively). Organisations are giving refuge to stay safely after the incidents. They also provide social support group and therapeutic counselling in several languages while in refuge. At the same time they give information and advice to all the victims and survivors regardless of gender and ethnicity. To prevent the forced marriage, government enacted the Forced Marriage (Civil Protection) Act 2007. The FMU are also communicating the message and providing services to all the relevant organisations. However, the study found, more than one-third organisations (37.5%) have 20 or more staff including male and female to deal with forced marriage and/ or relevant domestic violence. That makes them support the victims easily by establishing good rapport regardless of gender.

Nevertheless, women fleeing domestic violence desperately need emergency accommodation, support and protection. Those subject to the 'No Recourse to Public Funds', because of their insecure immigration status cannot access any form of emergency accommodation, including refuges, as they are not able to claim housing benefit, income support and other state benefits. To help those women Southall Black Sisters introduced 'The No Recourse Fund' that covers the costs of emergency accommodation and other basic living expenses to enable women and children to access places of safety such as a refuge. On the other hand, there are few specialised refuges for LGBT victims such as Stonewall Housing, Albert Kennedy Trust, etc. If the victims have been granted either ILR or DLR, organisations facilitate their introduction to a supporting organisation so that they can be supported in obtaining Job seekers allowance and housing benefits. In case of children, where required organisations make referrals to *Save the Children* to refer the young person to their Befriending Unaccompanied Minors Project (B.U.M.P). They also make referrals to the *Red Cross* for their International Tracing and Message service where required.

5.3.2 Limitations

UK government set up FMU, initiated some support programmes and enacted laws regarding forced marriage. But still this study found government poor in communicating message about forced marriage and not active enough to minimise the problem. There are some organisations having a limited number of staff (starting from 2 to 10). In addition, they are either male or female. Interestingly, most of the organisations have no advocates who speak clients' languages. It is obviously a barrier to understand the clients. All of these features cause a serious inadequacy in serving the victims. Again, as homosexuality and bisexuality is an emerging reason behind forced marriage, organisations should emphasis on those victims. At the moment, there are only few organisations (8.69%) who mainly working with LGBT victims. Most importantly, people with NRPF, have a restriction on receiving those services based on public funds. There are only one or two organisations helping the victims with NRPF. Even the funds these organisations are giving for victims' accommodation and subsistence is too low to survive and for a limited period.

Above all, the existing support services in the public, private and voluntary sectors are not well resourced and effective enough to deal with forced marriage. Lack of awareness about the danger of forced marriage amongst youngsters and elders makes the environment worse. As a result, affected communities are not giving priorities within themselves to abolish this bad custom. Support related to housing, education and self esteem issues are highly reported as a gap in the existing services. The gaps in existing support services and limitations in communicating message about forced marriage made this problem a big issue. However, this study pointed out some major limitations and gaps:

i) Priorities are not given within affected communities,
ii) lack of awareness amongst victims about what help is available,
iii) Support with getting legal services,
iv) Support with housing, school, self esteem issues,
v) Lack of faith with support services and criminal justice,
vi) Lack of Asian advocates and language barriers,
vii) Victims with NRPF have restrictions in access,
viii) Fear from most of educational institutions of being culturally insensitive and fear of 'upsetting' school governors by displaying leaflets on their premises about the subject,
ix) Services are not culturally or religiously appropriate for all the communities,
x) Organisations are not well-equipped and well-funded to serve LGBT victims.

5.3.3 Recommendations

To remove the practice of forced marriage, the whole community should work together. Local councils along with educational and religious institutions should educate and aware the community against forced marriage. Government has to take initiatives to engage and educate the community about forced marriage. The community people, especially parents and family should know about the laws and programmes that government introduced against forced marriage and why. However, lots of recommendations came out from the study. To improve the existing services and to communicate message effectively there are some recommendations:

i) Government should educate public about the danger of forced marriage,
ii) National Curriculum can introduce the concept of forced marriage in schools under the course of citizenship.
iii) Placing leaflets in places of public use, e.g., GP surgeries, hospitals, etc.
iv) Advertisements on public transports,
v) Involve religious leaders. Imams can talk (in Khuthba) about the responsibility of parents and children along with

unacceptability of forced marriage in Islam during Jum'a prayer on Friday,

vi) Organisations would need to expose themselves to the community more broadly,

vii) FMU and all national organisations should work in grassroots level with community organisations by engaging local people,

viii) Use of TV channels and radio can work out,

ix) Improve the relationships between men and women, and between parents and children,

x) Above all, victims should look for the services so that they can get help.

Finally, respondents also appreciated this research by defining it as a part of awareness against such an evil custom in society. Few strongly recommended for arranging a workshop with the help of any local community organisation to share the findings of the research. The report also can be published for all those community people involved in order to educate them briefly.

Chapter 6

Conclusion

6.1 Review of Previous Sections

This book is based on the study conducted on forced marriage to understand the nature and types of existing social work services and to evaluate how effective they are. In order to study this area, the circumstances of forced marriage were investigated through British Bangladeshi community. The first chapter includes background of the study, interest and motivation to research, research questions and hypothesis, aims and objectives and rationale for the research approach and methods chosen. Then, the second chapter drawn a context through literature review and established a theoretical framework for the study. Methodology for the study has been described in chapter three. The study has used survey and interviews as methods under a large qualitative approach with a small statistical analysis. Ethical issues involved in this research also discussed in that chapter. In chapter four, the original data were presented and later in chapter five the findings were discussed in relation to the context and theoretical framework. Finally, the concluding chapter composites a summary of main findings and evaluate their implications in the relevant area of international social work practice, policy and theory.

6.2 Summary of the main Findings

Forced marriage is when some one being asked to marry regardless of his or her choices and wishes. This practice is different from those of arranged marriage. South Asian minorities, specifically Bangladeshi community is vulnerable to economic downturn, regional variations and sectoral shifts in the labour market. Their low human capital leads to greater dependence on bonding social capital, which in turn, reinforces kin networks. On the other hand, as majority people are Muslim, Muslim identity also becoming more significant than ethnic identity. In terms of marriage, this is reflected by the view that cultural factors are less significant than religious ones. However, the study found many causes behind forced marriage including stronger relation build up within same families and preventing relationships outside the specific groups. Homophobia and controlling unwanted behaviour are other emerging causes of forced marriage. Although the religion of Islam prohibits forced marriage blaming religion became a common factor in forced marriage. This is because of the lack of education in the sense of their religious requirements and obligations.

There is debate about the numbers of forced marriage but it is clear that the problem is existing and that can partially explained by the demographic profile of Bangladeshi community: they have very young populations who are reaching marriageable age. And probably in this community, the institution of marriage is highly visible than some other communities. So statistically where the rate of marriage is high the possibility to find numbers of forced marriage could be higher than others. However, the study found one fifth of total victims are from British Bangladeshi community. Some one regardless of gender can be forced into marry even after the age of 30 though most of the victims are 18-22 years old and female. Giving information and advice, advocacy and counselling and providing refuge are the main support services available for the victims of forced marriage. Campaign programmes and involving young people in workshops about forced marriage are some of the preventive activities initiated by the relevant organisations to protect the potential victims. It is found that women and children are the main priority group for the service providers. Although government is working and enacted laws to minimise forced marriage, this study found government poor in doing so. Existing supports related to housing and education issues are not up to the mark to help the victims. In addition, organisations are not well equipped and well funded to serve the specific victims such as some one from LGBT community. Finally, communities are not giving priorities within themselves to identify the causes and not working hard to abolish this bad custom.

Government has to make sure that the whole community is engaged while studying, planning or implementing strategies to abolish forced marriage. Involving religious leaders and introducing forced marriage in school curriculum can make a huge difference. All relevant organisations should work in grassroots level with local community organisations by engaging and recruiting local people.

6.3 Implications in the Relevant Area of International Social Work

Forced marriage is not merely an issue in the UK. It is an International issue comes along with others like 'domestic violence', 'inequality', 'human rights', and 'poverty'. It can affect particular population globally and locally. International social work allows professionals to see that 'global issues' matter to this profession. In fact, it becomes an 'international' perspective on social work practice when a social work practice influenced by internationally related domestic practice and advocacy and international policy development (Healy, 2001:7). The exchanges of ideas by social workers at inter-country work and inter-governmental work can increase understanding of global events, influences and problems. Recognising the international and cross-cultural dimensions of local issues, utilising comparative or internationally derived knowledge to inform their analyses of problem areas and evaluation of possible strategies for intervention among social workers are core to international social work practice, theory and policy. This study addresses the international and cross-cultural dimensions of a social problem.

The successful partnerships that have been established between the British, Pakistani, Indian and Bangladeshi governments to combat forced marriage confirm that hatred for this practice is as strong outside the United Kingdom as within. Britain's record on enforcing human rights may be better than many other countries but still patchy in practice. Nevertheless, it is a fundamental feature of international practice based on a commitment to universal human rights that no groups or individuals can opt out of this commitment on cultural, traditional or any other illegitimate grounds. Based on a recent UK policy of providing protection for all British passport holders overseas (including who have dual nationality), south Asian governments assisting British victims of forced marriage abroad. Simply, 'think global—act social' is the main theme of this policy that relates international social work practice, theory and policy to this field. To work at local and global levels and to relate the two to diminish the social problems like forced marriage this study could be an important piece of evidence. Finally, the demands of women and minority ethnic groups, as well as the voices of younger, older and disabled people and the influence of social movements concerned with issues of sexuality and gender must all be taken into account in the construction of a social and global policy for this 21st century.

(APPENDIX—1)

About The Research

You are invited to take part to fill up this questionnaire for a study being conducted by myself, Abu Maruf, a postgraduate student of the School of Humanities and Social Sciences, University of East London. The purpose of the study is to know ***the nature and types of existing social work services and how effective they are to minimise forced marriage*** through British Bangladeshi community. The research is being conducted as a dissertation study for my MA in *International Social Work and Community Development*. I, as a researcher, will treat all survey materials as confidential.

Please Use This Section to Tell Me about Yourself

Full name:

Job title:

Date:

Name of the organisation:

Address:

Postcode:

Phone Number:

E-mail:

If you have any question about the study at any time, you are welcome to contact the researcher.

Thank you.

Abu Maruf
Postgraduate Student
University of East London (Docklands Campus)
4-6 University Way, London E16 2RD, UK.
Phone: *Removed for publication purposes*
Mobile: *Removed for publication purposes*
Email: *Removed for publication purposes*

Section One:

Circumstances of Forced Marriage

1) According to your record which particular South Asian ethnic group shows the maximum practice of forced marriage? (***CHOOSE ONE***)

   i)   Pakistanis   ii) Bangladeshis
   iii) Indians   iv) Other, (Please write below)

   _____

2) According to your statistics what is the current percentage (%) of British Bangladeshi victims of forced marriage?
   _____ *(APPROXIMATELY)*

3) How old were the majority victims? Average age ranged— (***CHOOSE ONE)***

   i)   From 13-17 years old   ii) From 18-22 years old
   iii) From 23-27 years old   iv) Other, (Please write below)

   _____

4) Does your organisation deal with more or less cases this year than last year?

   i)   More   ii) Less

5) What do you think the main reasons behind forced marriage? (***SELECT MAJOR THREE)***

   i)   Long-standing family commitments and preserving family honour
   ii) Assisting claims for UK residence and citizenship
   iii) Achieving financial gain

iv) Ensuring land, property and wealth remain within the family

v) Please state other reasons from the organisation's experience below

_____

Section Two:

Existing Social Work Services

6) Please specify the groups from the following to whom you serve in response to forced marriage? (*SELECT ALL THAT APPLY*)
   i) Adult female
   ii) Adult male
   iii) Both adult male and female
   iv) Children
   v) Disable
   vi) Some one from lesbian, gay, bisexual and trans-gendered (LGBT) community
   vii) Other voluntary organisations

7) How did you get your clients? (*SELECT MAJOR THREE*)
   i) Referred by Forced Marriage Unit (FMU)
   ii) Referred by educational institutions
   iii) Referred by any other professionals
   iv) Clients come directly through media (internet, newspaper, magazine, social journal, billboards, etc)
   v) Referred by client's friend
   vi) Other, please write below

_____

8) What sort of services you have for the victims of forced marriage? *(SELECT ALL THAT APPLY)*
   i)   Giving information and advice
   ii) Advocacy and counselling
   iii) Legal advice and representations
   iv) Refuge
   v)   Other, please write below

   _____

9) What sort of preventive activities you have initiated to minimise the forced marriage in the community? *(SELECT ALL THAT APPLY)*
   i)   Educating teachers, community workers, health professionals and all other relevant personnel about the issues surrounding forced marriage and the presenting symptoms
   ii) Circulating and displaying relevant information
   iii) Sticker, leaflets, billboards etc. on important places including train/bus stations and all other public transports
   iv) Involve young people by arranging workshops about forced marriage
   v)   Other, please write below

   _____

Section Three:

Evaluation

10) How many staff do you have to deal with forced marriage cases?
   _____ *(APPROXIMATELY)*

11) Do you have both male and female caseworkers/support workers to deal with the cases?

    i) Yes   ii) No

12) What do you feel about the gaps in existing services? (**SELECT ALL THAT APPLY**)

i)   Support with getting legal services

ii)   Victims with 'No recourse to public funds' have restrictions in access

iii)   Support with: housing, school, self esteem issues

iv)   Lack of faith with support services and criminal justice

v)   Lack of Asian advocates

vi)   Anything else (Please write below)

————

13) What are your recommendations/suggestions to improve the communication to support the forced marriage victims? (**SELECT ALL THAT APPLY**)

    i)   TV campaigns

    ii)   Radio including Asian networks

    iii)   Information at places of worship/ involve religious leaders

    iv)   Schools and colleges can introduce forced marriage into the curriculum by discussing different types of marriage (love matches, arranged and forced marriages) within relevant classes

    v)   Anything else, (Please write below)

————

Thank you for filling up this questionnaire.

Your signature: Date:

(APPENDIX—2)

You are invited to take part in an interview study being conducted by myself, Abu Maruf, a postgraduate student of the School of Humanities and Social Sciences, University of East London. The purpose of the study is ***to know the nature and types of existing social work services and how effective they are to minimise forced marriage*** through British Bangladeshi community. The research is being conducted as a dissertation study for my MA in *International Social Work and Community Development*.

The interview will last up to an hour, and will be recorded and transcribed. It will be at a time and place to suit you. Interview transcripts will be available if you want them, as will copies of papers emerging from the study. Transcripts and video/audio will be stored at my personal collection room as my research record for use in research and report writing, under a set of ethics agreed by the University Ethics Committee.

In this study:

> ➤ The researcher will treat all interview materials as confidential.
> ➤ Each interview audio/video and transcript will be given a code number to protect its anonymity.

> ➤ The research, including references to and quotations from interviews used in written papers and spoken presentations, will preserve interviewees' anonymity. All potentially identifying personal or institutional references will be removed carefully from transcripts.
> ➤ If there is an opportunity/necessity to use any reference or in case of publication researcher will ask you specifically about and get permission from you for this.
> ➤ Interviewees are all volunteers. They can stop the interview at any time, or refuse to answer any question.

If you have any question about the study at any time, you are welcome to contact the researcher.

Thank you.

Abu Maruf
Postgraduate Student
University of East London (Docklands Campus)
4-6 University Way, London E16 2RD, UK.
Phone: *Removed for publication purposes*
Mobile: *Removed for publication purposes*
Email: *Removed for publication purposes*

(APPENDIX—3)

Study on Forced Marriage

I have read and understood the description of the study on Forced Marriage. I volunteer to take part. I give my permission for the interview which I am about to give for this study to be used for research purposes only (including research publications and reports and archiving), with strict preservation of anonymity. I understand that I am not obliged to take part, and that I am free to withdraw at any time during the interview.

Signature (any name):   Date:

(APPENDIX—4)

Interview about Forced Marriage

Code Number:

Length of Interview:

Time and Date:

Please circle the descriptions that apply to you: **Female   Male**

Age:

Profession/ Occupation:

Religion:

Thanks very much for your help.

(APPENDIX—5)

Semi Structured Interview Guidelines

(Common questions for all the interviewees)

1. What is your general understanding of forced marriage?
2. How do you differentiate forced marriage from those known as arranged marriage?
3. Does the concept of arranged marriage is disappearing?
4. Do the religion, culture, education, social class and factors like that have any affect in forced marriage?
5. What is your common perception regarding the causes behind forced marriage?
6. What sort of social work services are available that you know for the potential victims, victims and survivors of forced marriage?
7. Do you think the organisations giving the beneficiaries a choice of culturally appropriate support?
8. How complex it is to support some one from LGBT in compared to Heterosexual victims?
9. Does the community have a role in tackling FM? Who in the community should be involved?

10. What is your opinion about the existing law—Forced Marriage (Civil Protection) Act 2007 and its effectiveness?
11. How effective has the Government been in communicating message about forced marriage?
12. Do you think the existing support services in the public, private and voluntary sectors are adequate, well resourced and effective in dealing with forced marriage cases?
13. How difficult it could be to access in services by the victims with ILE, ILR, DLR, ELR and NRPF?
14. What would be the most effective ways of raising community awareness about the unacceptability of forced marriage?
15. Do you have any further comments or suggestions about the concept of Forced Marriage and for this study?

(Few more questions asked to the survivors only)

1. How and where the story began?
2. What was the age and social/educational status at the time of incidence?
3. Where did you seek help and how they helped you?
4. How is the relation with parents/family now?
5. How do you find the life as a survivor?

(APPENDIX—6)

List of some important materials used as gifts during interview:

1. Forced Marriage Card
   Available from:
   http://www.fco.gov.uk/resources/en/pdf/travel-living-abroad/when-things-go-wrong/fm-card.pdf [15 Oct 2010]

2. Poster (English) on Forced Marriage
   Available from:
   http://www.fco.gov.uk/resources/en/pdf/forced-marriage-poster-english [15 Oct 2010]

3. Poster (English and Bengali, Size A2) on Forced Marriage
   Available from:
   http://www.fco.gov.uk/resources/en/pdf/forced-marriage-poster-bengali [15 Oct 2010]

4. Leaflet—'What is a Forced Marriage?'
   Available from:
   http://www.fco.gov.uk/resources/en/pdf/2855621/what-is-forced-marriage [15 Oct 2010]

(The printed copies of above materials were provided by the Forced Marriage Unit)

Glossary

Bongsho
'Bongsho' is often used to mean clan in Bengali. A clan is a group of people united by actual or perceived kinship and descent.

Endogamy
Marrying within a clan or tribe.

Ghusti
'Ghusti' is used to mean patrilineages in Bangladesh. Patrilineage is a group of descendants related through a common male (father) lineage.

Imam
An 'Imam' is the worship leader of a mosque who leads Islamic worship services. More often, Muslims turn to the mosque Imam for religious advocacy and counselling.

Insider
A member of a specified group/community who has special knowledge and access to confidential information. Here the author is an insider for the concerned community.

Jum'a Prayer
Jum'a is a congregational prayer that Muslims hold every Friday, just after noon in lieu of dhuhr (usual noon prayer). During this prayer largest number of Muslims gathers in mosques.

Khandhan
Extended family consists of kinship ties.

Khuthba
'Khuthba' is religious narration (including sermons) that may be pronounced in a variety of settings and at various times. Here it refers to khutbat al-jum'a, usually delivered in the mosque on every Friday during Jum'a Prayer.

Lascar
'Lascar' is sailor. A seaman, who navigates ships or assists in their operation, maintenance and service.

Peace Be Upon Him (PBUH)
Peace Be Upon Him is a phrase that practising Muslims say and expect from others to say after saying (or hearing) the name of a prophet of Islam.

Survivors
Here 'survivors' are those people who have passed the incidence of forced marriage and now living their life by escaping from that marriage.

Zat
'Zat' is caste or caste-like group in Bangladesh. It has the same meaning to all Bangladeshis living around the world.

Resources

A list of key organisations offering help and advice in response to Forced Marriage in the UK—

◆ Ashiana Project (London)
Telephone: 020 8539 0427
www.ashiana.org.uk

◆ Ashiana (Sheffield)
Telephone: 0114 255 5740
www.ashianahelp.org.uk

◆ Asian Women's Resource Centre (London)
Telephone: 020 8961 6549
www.asianwomencentre.org.uk

◆ Forced Marriage Unit
Telephone: 020 7008 0151
Email: fmu@fco.gov.uk
Email for outreach work: fmuoutreach@fco.gov.uk

◆ Gatwick Travel Care (Advice for victims of forced marriage requiring assistance)
Telephone: 01293 504283

◆ Ghar se Ghar
Asian and other minority ethnic women's support group (Information, Advice, Referral and Support)
C/O Bury Park Community Resource Centre, Dunstable Road, Luton.
Telephone: 01582 450194

◆ Heathrow Travel Care (Advice for victims of forced marriage requiring assistance)
Telephone: 020 8745 7495

◆ Henna Foundation (Cardiff)
Telephone: 029 2049 6920
www.hennafoundation.org

◆ Honour Network (Karma Nirvana)
Telephone: 0800 5999 247
www.karmanirvana.org.uk

◆ LIFE Project (Birmingham)
Telephone: 0121 554 3920
www.throughcare.com

◆ Muslim Women's Helpline (Information, Advice, Counselling), London
Telephone: 020 89048193/8908 6715

◆ National Domestic Violence Helpline (24 Hour Information, Advice, Referral and Support)
Telephone: 0808 200 0247

◆ Newham Asian Women's Project (London)
Telephone: 0208 472 0528
www.nawp.org

◆ NSPCC {Asian Child Protection Helpline (free confidential Information, Advice, Counselling)}
Telephone: 0800 096 7719

◆ Roshni (Nottingham Asian Women's Aid)
Telephone: 0115 948 3450, 24 hour
www.womensaid.org.uk

◆ Shakti Women's Aid (Edinburgh)
Telephone: 0131 475 2399
www.shaktiedinburgh.co.uk

◆ Southall Black Sisters (London)
Telephone: 020 8571 9595
www.southallblacksisters.org.uk

Bibliography

Asian Women's Resource Centre (2005) *Forced Marriage: Service User Consultation Report*, London: AWRC.

Blaxter, L., Hughes, C. & Tight, M. (2006) *How to Research,* 3rd edn. London: Open University Press.

Bradburn, N. M., Sudman, S. & Associates (1979) *Improving Interview Method and Questionnaire Design*, London: Jossey-bass Publishers.

Corbetta, P. (2003) *Social Research: Theory, Methods and Techniques,* London, Thousands Oak & New Delhi: Sage Publications.

Daryabadi, A.M. (2008) *The Glorious Qur'an: Text, Translation & Commentary*, Leicester: The Islamic Foundation.

Eversley, J. & Khanom, H. (2001) *Forced Marriages in the Bangladeshi Community: a Preliminary Report,* Queen Mary University of London: Public Policy Research Unit.

Foreign and Commonwealth Office (2004) *Young People and Vulnerable Adults Facing Forced Marriage: Practical Guidance for Social workers,* London: Home Office.

Gardner, K. (1995) *Global Migrants, Local Lives: Travel and Transformation in Rural Bangladesh*, Oxford: Clarendon Press.

Healy, L. (2001) *International Social Work: Professional Action in an Interdependent World*, Oxford & New York: Oxford University Press.

Home Office (2000) *A Choice by Right: the Report of the Working Group on Forced Marriage*, London: Home Office.

Khanum, N. (2008) *Forced Marriage, Family Cohesion and Community Engagement: National Learning through a Case Study of Luton*, Luton: Equality in Diversity.

Kazimirski, A., Keogh, P., Kumari, V., Smith, R., Gowland, S. & Purdon, S. with Khanum, N. (2009) *Forced Marriage—Prevalence and Service Response*, London: National Centre for Social Research.

Langan, M. & Day, L. (eds) (1992) *Women, Oppression and Social Work*, London: Routledge Publication.

Maruf, A. S. (Unpublished), *An Evaluation of Existing Social Work Services on Forced Marriage: A Study on British Bangladeshi Community*, submitted to the School of Humanity and Social Sciences at University of East London, UK as a dissertation for the MA in International Social Work and Community Development in January 2011.

Meenakshi, T. (2005) *Transnational Migration and the Politics of Identity*, London: Sage Publications.

Rowson, R. (2006) *Working Ethics: How to be Fair in a Culturally Complex World*, London & Philadelphia: Jessica Kingsley Publishers.

Samad, Y., Eade, J. & University of Surrey Roehampton (2002) *Community Perceptions of Forced Marriage*, Bradford and Surrey: Community Liaison Unit.

Seale, C. (ed) (1998) *Researching Society and Culture*, London: Sage Publications.

Seidman, I. (2006) *Interviewing as Qualitative Research: a Guide for Researchers in Education and the Social Sciences*, 3rd edn. New York: Teachers College Press.

Sudman, S. & Bradburn, N. M. (1982) *Asking Questions: a Practical Guide to Questionnaire Design*, London: Jossey-Bass Publishers.

Wengraf, T. (2001) *Qualitative Research Interviewing*, London: Sage Publications.

Online Sources: (sorted by access date)

1. Official website of "Foreign and Commonwealth Office"
    Available from:
    http://www.fco.gov.uk/en/travel-and-living-abroad/
    when-things-go-wrong/forced-marriage/ [30 April 2010]

2. Chantler, K., Gangoli, G. and Hester, M. (2009) *Forced marriage in the UK: Religious, Cultural, Economic or State Violence?* [Online] Critical Social policy.
    Available from:
    http://csp.sagepub.com/cgi/content/abstract/29/4/587 [01 May 2010]

3. 'A glimpse of the UK Bangladeshi community' in *New Age*
    Available from:
    http://www.newagebd.com/2007/jan/16/oped.html [02may 2010]

4. 'Bengali-speaking community in the Port of London' in *PortCities UK*
    Available from:
    http://www.portcities.org.uk/london/server/show/
    ConNarrative.126/chapterId/2600/Bengalispeaking-community-
    in-the-Port-of-London.html [02 May 2010]

5. 'History of Islam in the UK: Before the 20th Century' in *BBC News*
    Available from:
    http://www.bbc.co.uk/religion/religions/islam/history/uk1.shtml
    [02 May 2010]

6. 'Resident population estimates by Ethnic Group' in website of "Office for National Statistics"
Available from:
http://www.neighbourhood.statistics.gov.uk/dissemination/LeadTrendView.do?
a=3&b=276772&c=tower+hamlets&d=13&e=13&f=21810&g=346968&i=1001x1003x1004x1005&l=1809&o=198&m=0&r=1&s=1218827780554&enc=1&adminCompId=21810&variableFamilyIds=6286&xW=1014 [02 May 2010]

7. Information on Forced Marriage
Available from:
http://www.fco.gov.uk/en/travel-and-living-abroad/when-things-go-wrong/forced-marriage/info-for-professionals [30 Sep 2010]

8. A film—'What is Forced Marriage?'
Available from:
http://www.youtube.com/watch?v=AoGwwlFw20s [30 Sep 2010]

9. Multi-agency Practice Guidelines: Handling cases of Forced Marriage
Available from:
http://www.fco.gov.uk/resources/en/pdf/3849543/forced-marriage-guidelines09.pdf [05 Oct 2010]

10. The Right to Choose: Multi-agency Statutory Guidance for Dealing with Forced Marriage
Available from:
http://www.fco.gov.uk/resources/en/pdf/3849543/forced-marriage-right-to-choose [05 Oct 2010]

11. Survivor's Handbook
Available from:
http://www.fco.gov.uk/resources/en/pdf/travel-living-abroad/when-things-go-wrong/survivors-handbook [05 Oct 2010]

12. Leaflet—'What is a Forced Marriage?'
    Available from:
    http://www.fco.gov.uk/resources/en/pdf/2855621/
    what-is-forced-marriage [15 Oct 2010]

13. Poster (English and Bengali, Size A2) on Forced Marriage
    Available from:
    http://www.fco.gov.uk/resources/en/pdf/forced-marriage-poster-
    bengali [15 Oct 2010]

14. Forced Marriage Card
    Available from:
    http://www.fco.gov.uk/resources/en/pdf/travel-living-abroad/
    when-things-go-wrong/fm-card.pdf [15 Oct 2010]

15. Poster (English)
    Available from:
    http://www.fco.gov.uk/resources/en/pdf/forced-marriage-poster-
    english [15 Oct 2010]

16. Official website of "Southall Black Sisters"
    Available from:
    http://www.southallblacksisters.org.uk/ [10 Nov 2010]

17. Official website of "Women's Aid"
    Available from:
    http://www.womensaid.org.uk/ [10 Nov 2010]

18. Official website of "The Islamic Foundation"
    Available from:
    http://www.islamic-foundation.org.uk/User/Home.aspx [15 Nov
    2010]

19. Merriam-Webster Dictionary
    Available from:
    http://mw1.m-w.com/dictionary/marriage [05 Dec 2010]

20. A photograph of "Forced Marriage"
Available from:
http://www.fco.gov.uk/en/travel-and-living-abroad/
when-things-go-wrong/forced-marriage/ [05 Dec 2010]

21. Official website of "Channel S"
Available from:
http://www.chsuk.tv/ [05 Dec 2010]

22. 'Can a woman be forced into marriage in Islam?'—An online article
Available from:
http://www.answering-christianity.com/cant_force_marriage.htm
[05 Dec 2010]

Index

social workers, 2, 61
society, 14, 50, 57
solution, 4, 40, 51
son, 46
Southall Black Sisters, 43, 54
South Asian, 8-9, 17, 20, 25-6,
    49-50, 60, 62
spouses, 6, 38, 49
staff, 33, 52, 54-5
stakeholders, 16, 18-9
statements, 4, 18
status, 7, 9, 11, 14, 40, 43, 54
sticker, 32-3, 53
Stonewall Housing, 43, 54
strategies, 42, 61
students, 18
Study, 2-4, 9, 12, 14-7, 20, 22-3, 37,
    45, 47, 49-50, 52-6, 59-62
success, 3, 54
suicide, 6
superstitions, 39, 50
support services, 18, 31, 36, 41-2, 52,
    55-6, 60
support workers, 33-4, 50
survey, 12, 16-7, 19, 22, 25, 59
survivors, 2-3, 16, 18-9, 21, 31, 45,
    52-4
Sylhet, 8-9, 41
Sylheti cooks, 8

teachers, 18, 32, 53
techniques, 19
Thapan, 8
theoretical framework, 13-4, 49, 59
theory, 13, 59, 61-2
tradition, 8-9, 14, 38, 40
traditional, 2, 5, 7, 20, 38-9, 50, 62
training, 12, 45, 51

triangulation, 19
tribe, 40
TV channels, 57
twentieth century, 8

UK, 1, 8-9, 11, 17, 20, 26, 28-9,
    40-41, 43-4, 46, 50, 55, 61-2
unhappiness, 6
Universal Declaration of Human
    Rights, 6
upsetting, 35-6, 56

valid, 6, 10
values, 2, 21
victims, 1-3, 9, 17-8, 26-7, 30, 31,
    33, 35-6, 41-2, 43-4, 50, 52,
    54-7, 60-62
violence, 1-2, 11, 20
virgin, 11
voluntarily, 6, 37
volunteers, 18
vulnerable, 13, 20-21, 54, 60

Wales, 7
widow, 11
wife, 5, 10
Wiseman, 22
women, 1, 2, 8-11, 13, 17, 20, 28,
    50-54, 57, 60, 62
Working Group, 6-7
workshops, 32-3, 42, 53, 60
world, 2, 5, 17, 41, 44, 51

young, 1, 32-3, 42, 53, 55, 60, 62
youth projects, 42, 52

zat, 9, 51